STEPHEN HAWKING
Understanding the Universe

CHILDREN'S PRESS ®
A Division of Grolier Publishing
New York / London / Hong Kong / Sydney
Danbury, Connecticut

DEDICATION

In memory of my father

PHOTO CREDITS

Cover, Miriam Berkley; 1, 3, AP/Wide World; 5,
David Malin/Anglo-Australian Observatory; 9,
Godrey Argent/Camera Press, London; 10, David
Malin/Anglo-Australian Observatory; 13, AP/Wide
World; 15, Homer Sykes/Camera Press, London; 17,
18, Mark Paternostro; 19, 21, AP/Wide World; 23, 24,
Miriam Berkley; 26, Colin Mason/London Features
International; 27, AP/Wide World; 28, Stewart
Mark/Camera Press, London; 29, Richard
Open/Camera Press, London; 31, AP/Wide World;
32, Dan Winters/The Walt Disney Company.
Reprinted with permission of *Discover* Magazine

EDITORIAL STAFF

Project Editor: Sarah DeCapua
Design and Electronic Composition: Biner Design Inc.
Photo Editor: Jan Izzo

Library of Congress Cataloging-in-Publication Data
Sakurai, Gail.
   Stephen Hawking : understanding the universe / by Gail
Sakurai.
      p. cm. — (Picture-story biographies)
   Includes index.
   Summary : A brief biography of the British theoretical
physicist who is well-known for his advances in the study
of cosmology, accomplished despite being physically
limited by amyotrophic lateral sclerosis (ALS) or Lou
Gehrig's disease.
   ISBN 0-516-04195-9 (lib. bdg.) – ISBN 0-516-20055-0 (pbk.)
   1. Hawking, S. W. (Stephen W.)—Juvenile literature.
2. Physicists—Great Britain—Biography— Juvenile
literature. [1. Hawking, S. W. (Stephen W.) 2. Physicists.
3. Physically handicapped.] I. Title. II. Series.

QC16.H33S24 1996
530.092—dc20
[B]   95-51019
                                                          CIP
                                                           AC

SEVERAL MEN SAT AROUND a green felt-covered table. They were playing poker and trading jokes about science. Three of the poker players were famous physicists — Isaac Newton, Albert Einstein, and Stephen Hawking. With a gleeful chuckle, Stephen Hawking flipped over his cards — four sevens and a jack. He had won the poker game against two of history's greatest scientific minds.

"Cut!" yelled the director, and the cameras stopped rolling.

Stephen Hawking (center) joins actors portraying Albert Einstein (left) and Sir Isaac Newton (right) during filming of "Star Trek: The Next Generation."

The poker game wasn't real. It was a scene filmed for the popular television show, "Star Trek: The Next Generation." Hollywood actors played the roles of Newton and Einstein. But the frail-looking man in the wheelchair was the real Stephen Hawking. He is the most famous scientist in the world today.

Stephen William Hawking was born on January 8, 1942, in Oxford, England. He was the oldest of four children. The Hawking family lived in London until 1950. Then, they moved to St. Albans, a town about twenty miles north of London.

Stephen was an active, curious boy. He loved toys with moving parts, especially model trains. He liked to take things apart to see how they worked. But, he wasn't very good at putting them back together. Stephen enjoyed building radio-controlled model boats and airplanes. His models often looked

Stephen's curiosity about the universe began with childhood play.

rough and unfinished, but that didn't bother Stephen. He only cared about how well they worked, not what they looked like.

Stephen didn't do very well in school, even though he was bright. He didn't learn to read until he was eight years old. His schoolwork was usually messy and full of mistakes. His handwriting was sloppy, and he rarely studied. At this early age, Stephen did not show many signs of future greatness.

5

When Stephen was twelve, one of his friends bet another friend a bag of candy that Stephen would never be a success. Years later, Stephen said, with typical humor, "I don't know if this bet was ever settled and, if so, which way it was decided."

Stephen's father was a doctor who did research in tropical diseases. He would have liked Stephen to become a doctor, too, but Stephen had no interest in medicine or biology. Stephen however, did find scientific research interesting. He enjoyed visiting his father's laboratory and looking through the microscopes.

It seemed natural to Stephen to follow in his father's footsteps and to choose a career in scientific research. By the time he was fourteen, Stephen had decided that he wanted to specialize in mathematics and physics. Physics is the study of matter and energy and the scientific laws that govern their behavior. Dr. Hawking worried that Stephen would not be able to find a good job in the field of mathematics. He persuaded his son to study mostly science and only a little math.

Stephen thought physics was the easiest, most boring subject at school. He found chemistry class much more interesting and exciting because unexpected things, such as explosions, can often happen. In spite of this, Stephen decided to specialize in physics because he wanted to know how things worked. He thought that physics would provide the best chance of understanding the universe.

Both of Stephen's parents had attended Oxford University. Stephen wanted to go there, too. He applied to Oxford when he was only seventeen years old. To everyone's surprise, Stephen did so well on the entrance exam that he won a scholarship to study physics at Oxford.

At first, Stephen was lonely at Oxford. He felt out of place because he was younger than the other students. After a while, he began to make friends. He joined the rowing team and became coxswain of his eight-man crew. The coxswain is the person who steers the boat.

Stephen didn't change his poor study habits while at Oxford. In fact, he only worked at his studies for about one hour a day. It was easy for Stephen to avoid work at the university. No one forced him to attend classes or complete assignments. There were no grades or tests until the end of the three-year program. Fortunately for Stephen, he was very intelligent. In spite of not studying, he managed to pass the final exam and receive a first-class degree.

Stephen graduated from Oxford in 1962, when he was twenty years old. Then, he went to Cambridge University to begin graduate studies in cosmology. Cosmology is the branch of physics that deals with the nature of the universe, how it was formed, and how it will end. Stephen planned to earn a Ph.D., also known as a doctorate. This is the most advanced degree available.

Stephen developed ALS at the age of twenty-one.

At Cambridge, Stephen noticed he was becoming clumsy. He sometimes stumbled and fell. Tasks that had been easy, such as tying his shoes or writing, were becoming difficult. These problems had actually started during his final year at Oxford, but Stephen had not paid much attention to them at that time.

When Stephen returned home from Cambridge during the Christmas holidays, his mother realized that something was wrong with him. She took Stephen to the doctor. The doctor sent him to the hospital for two weeks of

Cosmology is the study of the universe.

medical testing. The test results were shocking.

Stephen had an incurable disease called amyotrophic lateral sclerosis, or ALS. The doctor told him that he had only two years to live.

In the United States, ALS is often called Lou Gehrig's disease, after the famous baseball player who died of it. In England, it is known as motor neurone disease. ALS usually strikes people who are between forty and sixty years old. Stephen had just turned twenty-one.

ALS destroys the nerves that control the body's muscles. The muscles gradually grow weaker and become paralyzed. At first, Stephen would be able to use a cane to get around. As his muscles became weaker, he would need to use a wheelchair.

ALS does not affect thinking or memory. Stephen would remember, see, hear, taste, and smell the same as he always did. But soon he would be unable to walk, talk, write, or do even the simplest tasks for himself.

Stephen became deeply depressed. He spent long hours alone in his room, listening to classical music and reading science fiction. He saw no point in studying. He didn't expect to live long enough to finish his doctorate. It was a very sad time for Stephen Hawking.

Then, several things happened to pull Stephen out of his despair. The progress of his disease slowed down, and it appeared that he would live longer than he first thought. He became interested in his studies. And he fell in love with a bright, energetic college student named Jane Wilde.

Stephen and Jane wanted to get married. Stephen said, "If we were to get married, I had to get a job. And to get a job, I had to finish my Ph.D. I started

Stephen with his first wife, Jane

working hard for the first time in my life. To my surprise, I found I liked it."

Before Stephen got ALS, he had been bored with life; nothing had seemed worth doing. ALS changed his attitude. "When you are faced with the possibility of an early death," Stephen said, "it makes you realize that life is worth living and that there are lots of things you want to do."

Stephen applied for a teaching job at Cambridge University. He was hired as a Research Fellow, or professor, at Cambridge's Gonville and Caius College.

Stephen decided he was lucky to have chosen physics for his career. Although ALS would slowly paralyze his body, it would not affect his brain. As a physicist, he could do all his work in his head.

Stephen Hawking and Jane Wilde were married in July 1965. For their first year of marriage, Jane attended college classes in London during the week. She joined Stephen in Cambridge on the weekends. Although she was busy with her own studies, Jane typed Stephen's thesis for him. A thesis is a long research paper required to earn a doctorate. In 1966, Jane graduated from college, and Stephen received his Ph.D.

Stephen and Jane Hawking soon decided to start a family. Their first child, Robert, was born in 1967. Their daughter, Lucy, followed three years later. Timothy came along in 1979.

Jane put aside any plans for her own career. She devoted herself to taking care of the house, the children, and Stephen. Jane's efforts gave Stephen the chance to spend all his time and energy on physics. He never had to help with household chores or child care. After all, if he had trouble feeding and dressing himself, how could he feed or dress a baby? Jane joked that unlike other wives, she wasn't surprised or upset when her husband didn't help around the house.

Stephen and Jane Hawking and their children, Robert (standing), Lucy (left), and Timothy (in Stephen's lap)

Most of Stephen's early work in physics was on black holes. A black hole is an invisible object in space with such powerful gravity that nothing, not even light, can escape from it. A black hole can form when a very large star uses up all of its fuel and collapses.

When Stephen started his work in physics, black holes were just an interesting scientific idea. There was no proof that they actually existed. Then, in 1971, astronomers discovered a binary star system called Cygnus X-1. A binary star system is two stars orbiting around each other. Cygnus X-1 was unusual because one of its stars was invisible. But scientists realized they could locate the invisible star by the effect it had on its partner. The dark star was pulling hot, swirling gases off the visible star and creating a storm of X rays.

Today, most scientists are convinced that the dark star in Cygnus X-1 is a

An artist's version of a black hole

black hole. Possible black holes have been discovered in other binary systems, as well. Astronomers have also found evidence of extremely large black holes at the centers of some galaxies, including our own galaxy, the Milky Way.

Many of Stephen's ideas about black holes were new and surprising. For instance, in 1971, Stephen suggested that very tiny black holes could have formed right after the big bang. The big bang theory states that a gigantic explosion created the universe about fifteen billion years ago.

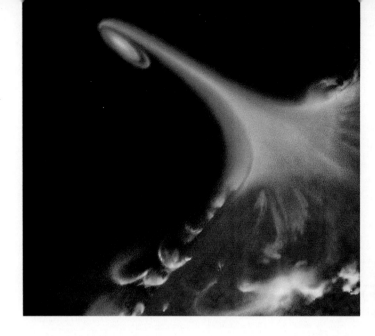

Cygnus X-1, which scientists believe contains a black hole

Then, in 1974, Stephen announced that black holes are not completely black. He had discovered that black holes give off radiation and gradually fade away. Eventually they disappear in a huge explosion. This idea was so astonishing that, at first, other scientists refused to believe it. When they checked Stephen's mathematical calculations themselves, however, they realized that he was correct. In the end, Stephen's discovery gained wide acceptance. Black hole radiation is now called "Hawking radiation" in his honor.

Eventually, Stephen expanded his work beyond black holes. He wanted to find answers to questions about the universe. He hoped to discover a single scientific theory that would explain the nature of the entire universe and everything in it.

One of Stephen's theories was called the no-boundary proposal. The no-boundary proposal suggested that the

Stephen delivers a speech about black holes.

universe was completely self-contained, with no beginning and no end. It simply existed.

Stephen became famous for his work in physics. He received many honors and awards. In 1974, he became a member of the Royal Society of Great Britain, a group of the best British scientists. He received the Albert Einstein Award for Theoretical Physics in 1978. Four years later, Queen Elizabeth II named him a Commander of the British Empire, one of the highest honors in Great Britain. Many colleges and universities awarded Stephen honorary degrees.

For all of Stephen's hard work, Cambridge University also rewarded him with several promotions. Finally, on April 29, 1979, Cambridge gave Stephen its most-honored position, called the Lucasian Professor of Mathematics. This post has been held by many of the most

Stephen (far right) received many important scientific awards as a result of his research.

well-known British scientists, including Sir Isaac Newton, who developed the theory of gravity.

It is traditional for the new Lucasian Professor of Mathematics to give a special talk, called an inaugural lecture. But, by this time, ALS caused Stephen's speech to be very slurred. Only the people who knew him well could still understand him. They would write down what he said, or repeat it out loud so others could understand, too. So, one of Stephen's students read his inaugural lecture for him.

Stephen also needed help with getting up, dressing, eating, and getting ready for bed. He had to use a motorized wheelchair because he could not walk. He couldn't even write with a pen or type on a computer. Stephen had to depend on other people to do things for him.

At first, Jane took care of Stephen all by herself. Later, as his condition grew worse, extra help was needed. Stephen and Jane began inviting one of Stephen's graduate students to live with the family. The student would help Stephen with personal hygiene tasks. In exchange, the student would receive free room and board, and a great deal of Stephen's time and personal attention. Students felt honored to be chosen to work so closely with Stephen Hawking, so it was a good arrangement for everyone.

Stephen did not let his disease stop him from enjoying life. He and Jane often attended concerts and plays. Stephen loved parties. He also liked to travel. Stephen made many trips to the United States, Canada, Russia, and other countries. He even rode his wheelchair on top of the Great Wall of China.

Stephen was receiving a lot of public attention. Many magazines and newspapers wrote articles about him. People admired him for what he had

As his disease grew worse, Stephen taught his lessons with help from students.

accomplished in spite of his illness. But Stephen refused to think of himself as a hero. "I get embarrassed when people say I have great courage," he said. "I have only done what I intended to do anyway, before I had ALS. I think the people with real courage are those worse affected but who don't get public attention or sympathy."

In 1985, while on a visit to Switzerland, Stephen became ill with pneumonia.

Stephen enjoys giving personal attention to his students.

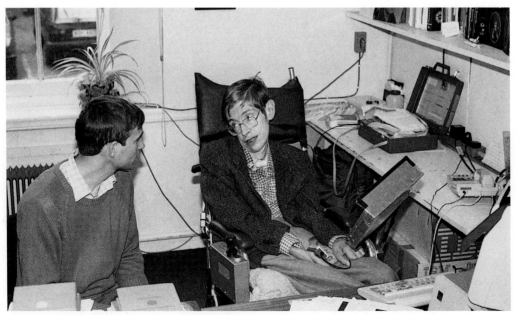

Pneumonia is a condition that affects the lungs and breathing passages. It is extremely dangerous for people with ALS. Stephen could not breathe; he was choking to death. Doctors had to perform emergency surgery. They created an opening in Stephen's throat and inserted a tube in the opening so he could breathe.

Unfortunately, the operation that saved Stephen's life took away his ability to speak. For a while, he spelled out words by raising his eyebrows when someone pointed to the correct letter on an alphabet card. This was a slow and tiring process. Stephen said, "It is pretty difficult to carry on a conversation like that, let alone write a scientific paper."

How could Stephen Hawking return to work? How could he teach a class, give a lecture, or finish the book he had started writing? The situation seemed hopeless.

The breathing tube inserted in Stephen's throat saved his life, but left him unable to speak.

Then, a computer expert in California heard about Stephen's problem. He sent Stephen a special computer program. The program let Stephen use his fingers to squeeze a control and to choose words from lists on a computer screen. A speech synthesizer connected to the computer "spoke" the words that Stephen selected. Later, Stephen had a small personal computer and a synthesizer connected to his wheelchair, so he could take his new voice everywhere with him.

With the computer and synthesizer, Stephen could write or speak fifteen words a minute. This is much slower than normal speech. Stephen joked, "I think slowly, so it [speaking slowly] suited me quite well." Although the new system was slow, Stephen could still communicate better than when his speech was so slurred. He said, "This system has made all the difference."

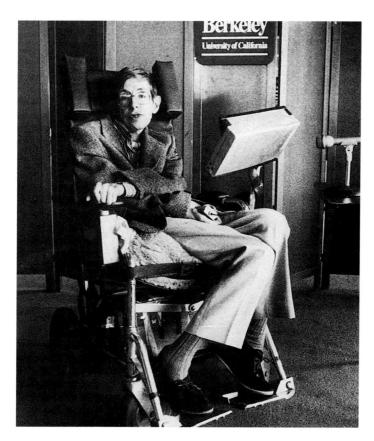

The speech synthesizer, connected to his wheelchair, allows Stephen to communicate freely.

Before he caught pneumonia, Stephen had started writing a science book for the general public. He was able to finish it with his new computer system. In the book, Stephen explained difficult physics concepts in simple ways, without using mathematical equations. He wanted to help nonscientists understand the work that he and other physicists were doing. Stephen's book, *A Brief History of Time: From the Big Bang to Black Holes*, was

Stephen shows a young person how to use a speech synthesizer.

Stephen with his best-selling book, A Brief History of Time

published in 1988. It quickly became a bestseller. It sold millions of copies and was translated into dozens of foreign languages. The book's success made Stephen even more famous than he was before.

After his operation, Stephen needed full-time nursing care. According to Stephen, this put a great strain on his marriage to Jane. As a result, Stephen and Jane Hawking separated in 1990. They later divorced.

In 1992, a Hollywood movie producer made a film about Stephen's life and work. The movie had the same title as Stephen's book: *A Brief History of Time*. Not only was Stephen a famous physicist and a best-selling author, now he was a movie star, too. The following year, he briefly became a television actor.

Stephen's television role came about during a trip to Los Angeles, California. While there, Stephen visited the Paramount film studios and toured the sets of "Star Trek: The Next Generation," one of his favorite television shows. Stephen was thrilled when he was allowed to sit in the captain's chair on the bridge of the starship, *Enterprise*. But an even greater thrill was in store.

Stephen was invited to make a guest appearance on "The Next Generation," in a scene written especially for him. In the scene, Stephen played poker in the starship's holodeck with the android character, Data. Two of history's greatest physicists, Isaac Newton and Albert Einstein, joined them.

Stephen has visited the imaginary future of "Star Trek"; but what does the real future hold for him? Stephen was remarried on September 15, 1995. He continues his work in physics, searching for new answers to age-old questions.

"My goal is simple," Stephen Hawking says. "It is a complete understanding of the universe."

In 1995, Stephen married his former nurse, Elaine Mason.

STEPHEN HAWKING

1942 January 8 — Stephen Hawking is born in Oxford, England
1962 Graduates from Oxford University
      Enters Cambridge University doctorate program
      Develops amyotrophic lateral sclerosis (ALS)
1965 Becomes Research Fellow at Gonville and Caius College
      Marries Jane Wilde
1966 Receives Ph.D. from Cambridge University
1967 Son, Robert, is born
1970 Daughter, Lucy, is born
1979 Becomes Lucasian Professor of Mathematics at Cambridge
      Son, Timothy, is born
1985 Falls ill with pneumonia; loses ability to speak
1988 Publishes book, *A Brief History of Time*
1990 Separates from wife, Jane; they later divorce
1992 Films movie version of *A Brief History of Time*
1993 Appears on "Star Trek: The Next Generation"
1995 Marries his nurse, Elaine Mason

INDEX

ABOUT THE AUTHOR

Gail Sakurai has had a lifelong interest in astronomy and space. When she was a child, she and her father used to stargaze with his homemade telescope. Nowadays, Ms. Sakurai lives in Cincinnati, Ohio, with her husband and two sons. When she is not researching or writing, she enjoys reading, traveling, and watching "Star Trek" on television. *Stephen Hawking: Understanding the Universe* is Gail Sakurai's fourth book for young readers. She is a full member of the Society of Children's Book Writers and Illustrators.